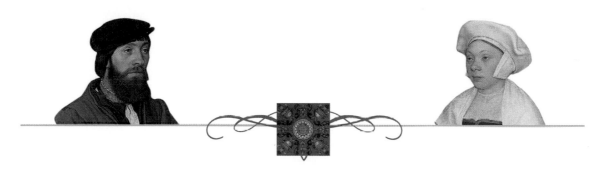

THE COURT

Life in the Renaissance
THE COURT

KATHRYN HINDS

BENCHMARK BOOKS
MARSHALL CAVENDISH
NEW YORK

To Fox, Margie, and Tamatha

Grateful acknowledgment is made to Monica Chojnacka, Associate Professor of History, University of Georgia, for her generous assistance in reading the manuscript.

Quote on p. 24 (duke of Urbino's palace) from Hale, p. 83. Quote on p. 24 (Medici palace) from *Rebirth of Genius*, p. 73. Quote on p. 24 (conveniences of Medici palace) from *Rebirth of Genius*, p. 72. Description of Sforza court on pp. 26–27 adapted from Mateer, p. 31. Quote on p. 39 (*The Courtier*) from Rowse, p. 63. Poem on pp. 40–41 ("Green Groweth the Holly") slightly adapted from *The Norton Anthology of Poetry, Revised*, edited by Alexander W. Allison et al. (New York: Norton, 1975), p. 77. Elizabeth's speech on p. 49 from *The Norton Anthology of Literature by Women: The Tradition in English*, edited by Sandra M. Gilbert and Susan Gubar (New York: Norton, 1985), p. 30. Quote on pp. 50–51 (*The Courtier*) from King, p. 188. Quote on p. 65 (Giovanni Pontano) from Kekewich, pp. 30–31.

All Shakespeare quotes are from *William Shakespeare, Complete Works, Compact Edition*, edited by Stanley Wells et al. (Oxford: Clarendon Press, 1988).

Benchmark Books
Marshall Cavendish
99 White Plains Road
Tarrytown, New York 10591-9001
www.marshallcavendish.com

Library of Congress Cataloging-in-Publication Data
Hinds, Kathryn, 1962-
The court / by Kathryn Hinds.
p. cm. — (Life in the Renaissance.)
Summary: Describes court life during the Renaissance, from about 1400 to 1600, explaining how various rulers governed and help shape European civilization.
Includes bibliographical references and index.
ISBN 0-7614-1676-5
1. Renaissance—Juvenile literature. 2. Courts and courtiers—Juvenile literature. 3. Europe—Kings and rulers—Juvenile literature. 4. Europe—Civilization—Juvenile literature. [1. Renaissance. 2. Courts and courtiers. 3. Kings, queens, rulers, etc. 4. Europe—Civilization.] I. Title. II. Series.
CB361.H56 2003
940.2'1'08621—dc21
2003001126

Art research by Rose Corbett Gordon, Mystic CT
Cover: Scala/Art Resource, NY
Page 1 (left & right), 38 & 62: Erich Lessing/Art Resource, NY; page 2: Victoria & Albert Museum/Bridgeman Art Library; page 10: Alinari/Art Resource, NY; page 13: Museo Real Academia de Bellas Artes, Madrid/Bridgeman Art Library; page 15: National Gallery, London/Bridgeman Art; page 16: Pelworth House, Sussex/Art Resource, NY; page19: Giraudon/Art Resource, NY; page 20: Staatliche Museen Kassel; page 22: Museo di Firenze Com'era, Florence/Bridgeman Art Library; page 23: Palazzo Ducale, Mantua/Bridgeman Art Library; page 27: J. Paul Getty Museum, Los Angeles/Bridgeman Art Library; page 28: National Portrait Gallery, London/Bridgeman Art Library; page 30: Hermitage, St. Petersburg/Bridgeman Art Library; page 34: Czartoryski Museum, Krakow/Bridgeman Art Library; page 41: Burghley House Collection, Lincolnshire/Bridgeman Art Library; page 44: Kunsthistorisches Museum, Vienna/Bridgeman Art Library; page 47: Church of the Assumption Duomo, Prato/Bridgeman Art Library; page 51: Kunsthistorisches Museum, Vienna/Bridgeman Art Library; page 53: Private Collection/Bridgeman Art Library; page 60: Musée des Beaux-Arts, Lille/Bridgeman Art Library; page 67: Fogg Art Museum, Harvard University Art Museums/Bridgeman Art Library; page 68: Art Resource, NY; pages 70 & 72: British Library/Bridgeman Art Library; page 71: British Library

Book design by Patrice Sheridan
Printed in China
1 3 5 6 4 2

cover: A young member of the ruling family of Florence, Italy, takes part in a procession with a tame cheetah at his side.
half title page: Portraits of a courtier and his wife from the court of King Henry VIII of England, painted by Hans Holbein the Younger.
title page: This detail from a fifteenth-century tapestry shows a richly attired nobleman and lady riding a horse together.

CONTENTS

ABOUT THE RENAISSANCE

W hen we talk about the Renaissance, we generally mean the period of western European history from roughly 1400 to 1600. The Renaissance can also be understood as a cultural movement in which art, literature, music, philosophy, and education shared in certain trends and influences. This movement had its origins in fourteenth-century Florence, Italy. Here the great writer Francesco Petrarca, or Petrarch, promoted the idea of a rebirth of the literature and learning of ancient Greece and Rome—*renaissance* means "rebirth."

This notion gradually spread throughout Italy and much of the rest of western Europe. As it did, people also grew interested in giving new life to Greek and Roman styles of art and architecture. In the process of rediscovering ancient culture and adapting it to the times, Renaissance people began to create unique cultures of their own. Many Europeans developed a great love of beauty, art, and learning for their own sake.

Some Renaissance thinkers felt that they were living at the dawn of a magnificent new era, leaving behind a time they considered "the dark ages." They believed that they would not only revive the glories of the ancient world, but surpass them. This belief seemed to be confirmed as new artistic techniques, architectural styles, philosophies, and educational practices caught on all over Europe. Historians now realize, however, that the seeds of these magnificent achievements were already present in medieval Europe. But although the

Renaissance did not make a total break with the past, three momentous changes occurred during this period that definitely paved the way to the modern age.

First was the invention of movable type and the printing press. Two German goldsmiths, Johannes Gutenberg and Johann Fust, invented movable type in 1446–1448. Then, between 1450 and 1455 Gutenberg used the world's first printing press to produce the world's first printed book, the famous Gutenberg Bible. Before this, all books had been written out and produced entirely by hand. They were therefore expensive and fairly rare. Since most people could not afford to own books, most people did not learn how to read. With the printing press, books—and the ideas and stories contained in them—became much more widely available.

Second, the Renaissance was a period when Europeans made many voyages of exploration. Explorers originally sought new and better routes to Asia, the source of silk, spices, and other goods that brought high prices in European markets. In 1492 the Italian explorer Christopher Columbus landed on the island of Hispaniola in the Caribbean. At first it was thought that this land was part of Asia. By 1500 it was clear that Columbus had reached a continent whose existence had been previously unknown to most Europeans. It was a true turning point in world history.

The third great change for western Europe was the Protestant Reformation. During the Middle Ages, western Europe had been united by one Church, headquartered in the ancient Italian city of Rome. In 1517 a monk named Martin Luther nailed a list of protests to a German cathedral door. Luther hoped to reform the Catholic Church, to purify it and rid it of corrupt practices. Instead, his action sparked the beginning of a new religious movement. Now there were many conflicting ideas about what it meant to be a Christian.

Renaissance people had many of the same joys and sorrows, hopes and fears that we do. They were poised at the beginning of the modern age, but still their world was very different from ours. Forget about telephones, computers, cars, and televisions, and step back into a time when printed books were a wonderful new thing. Let the Renaissance come alive. . . .

One

A VARIETY OF COURTS

I f you were to look at a map of Europe during the Renaissance, you probably would be surprised. Its borders would appear very different from the way they do today. Many nations that exist now were then just taking shape, or were divided into a number of independent states. Governments also took various forms, but all were dominated by people in the highest levels of society. Leaders came from ancient noble families or, in many cities, from wealthy merchant families. Most Renaissance states were headed by a single person—a nobleman, king, or, in a few cases, queen. To get a full picture of life at the courts of such rulers, it is helpful to first take a look at the world in which they ruled.

ON THE ITALIAN PENINSULA

Italy is considered the birthplace of the Renaissance. Yet Italy was not a unified nation during this period. Instead, the Italian peninsula was occu-

Giorgio Vasari—painter, architect, and art historian—decorated a palace wall with this portrait of Cosimo de' Medici, the unofficial ruler of Florence, surrounded by artists and philosophers. Like many Renaissance rulers and nobles, members of the Medici family used their wealth and influence to support learning and the arts.

pied by about 250 independent or semi-independent states. Most of these were city-states, in which one city not only governed itself but also ruled the surrounding region. Many city-states were quite small, but a few controlled considerable territory, including other cities as well as rural areas.

A large portion of northern Italy was part of the Holy Roman Empire. The empire was based in Austria, however, and the emperor usually left his Italian lands alone. City-states that were within the boundaries of the Holy Roman Empire were generally free to govern themselves. Much of central Italy was ruled by the pope, head of the Catholic Church. The area under his authority was called the Papal States, and its heart was the city of Rome. Some cities in the Papal States were basically independent, but in much of the area the pope had absolute control. Southern Italy belonged to the Kingdom of Naples, which was under Spanish rule for most of the Renaissance.

Many Italian city-states were republics, governed by committees of elected representatives. A number of the largest and most influential city-states, though, were ruled by a single nobleman, usually with the title of marquis or duke. When he died, his title and position passed to his oldest son or, if there was no son, to a brother or nephew.

The city-state of Florence began the Renaissance as a republic and ended it as a dukedom. In the beginning, eight hundred wealthy families made up the city's ruling class, but by the 1430s one family had come to dominate all the others. This was the Medici, who ran the largest bank in Europe. At first they exercised their power behind the scenes, then they more openly took charge of the government of Florence. Finally in the 1530s the Medici were recognized as hereditary dukes of Florence.

THE HOLY ROMAN EMPIRE

Nearly the whole German-speaking area of Europe was officially part of the Holy Roman Empire. The emperor was elected by a group of German noblemen. Beginning in 1438 the nobles always elected a member of the powerful royal family of the Habsburgs. The Habsburgs, especially Maximilian I, made the most of the grandeur and symbolic importance of being emperor, and the family became even stronger. Through a combination of warfare and marriages, the Habsburg influence eventually extended from Spain to Hungary.

In spite of the large amount of territory under the Holy Roman Emperors' control, they generally concentrated their attention on their domains in Austria and eastern Europe. The area that is now Germany was a jigsaw puzzle of more or less independent states. Some were ruled by hereditary princes, counts, or dukes. Others were basically city-states governed by elected mayors and councils. Many cities joined together in leagues, such as the Swabian League of southern Germany, to handle matters of both business and defense—including defense against too much control by the Holy Roman Emperor.

FRANCE, SPAIN, AND ENGLAND

Farther west in Europe, royal rule was becoming stronger. In France at the beginning of the Renaissance, nobles who governed large counties barely recognized the French king's authority over them. But in 1461 Louis XI became king and began a program to destroy the nobles' power. By making and breaking laws to suit his own purposes, seizing nobles' landholdings, and conquering those who tried to resist his authority, he brought nearly all of France firmly under his control within two decades. Louis made royal power absolute and unlimited in France.

A similar process occurred in Spain, where there were four distinct kingdoms: Navarre, Aragon, Castile, and Granada. The marriage of Ferdinand of Aragon and Isabella of Castile joined their two realms in 1469. In 1492 the royal pair conquered Granada, putting an end to seven centuries of Muslim rule in southern Spain. In 1512 Ferdinand took over

Holy Roman Emperor Maximilian I, Mary of Burgundy, and their family. Between the emperor and his wife stands their son Philip the Fair, who became king of Spain thanks to his marriage to Juana, the daughter of Queen Isabella and King Ferdinand. In the front center of this royal family portrait is Philip and Juana's son Charles, who would grow up to be king of Spain and the Holy Roman Emperor.

Navarre, making Spain all one kingdom. Ferdinand and Isabella began a line of powerful Spanish monarchs. Their grandson Charles became not only king of Spain but also Holy Roman Emperor, in addition to inheriting the Low Countries (modern Belgium, Luxembourg, and the Netherlands) and Burgundy (now eastern France) from his father, the duke of Burgundy.

Other nations, too, were headed by extraordinary rulers: King Henry VIII and Queen Elizabeth I of England, and King Francis I of France, stand out as some of the major figures of the age. Such monarchs resisted old tendencies to allow local governments almost complete independence. Instead, they held the reins of power firmly in their own royal hands. They promoted the idea of the state and its ruler being one and the same. Encouraging their subjects' loyalty to themselves, they also encouraged the strong development of a sense of nationhood.

The Other Empire

The invention of the printing press, the exploration of a previously unknown continent, the formation of rival Christian churches—these three events made an absolute break between Europe's medieval past and modern future. Europeans of the Renaissance would probably have added a fourth earth-shattering event to this list, and that was the conquest of Constantinople by the Ottoman Turks in 1453.

For more than a thousand years, Constantinople had been one of the greatest cities of the world. It had been the capital of the Byzantine Empire, the Greek-speaking successor of the eastern half of the ancient Roman Empire. It was also the center of Orthodox Christianity, the form of Christianity followed throughout most of eastern Europe. Constantinople was renowned for its size, wealth, and beauty. And its location was of huge strategic importance, for it sat on the Bosporus, a narrow strait that led from the Mediterranean Sea to the Black Sea. On one side lay Asia, and on the other Europe.

With the conquest of Constantinople, the Ottoman Empire was at Europe's doorstep. This was seen as not just a political threat but also a religious one, for the Ottoman Turks were Muslims. Western European rulers, especially the popes and the Holy Roman Emperors, felt the pressure of Ottoman expansion throughout the Renaissance. There were several attempts to unite various European countries in war against the Turks, but these were mostly unsuccessful. By 1530 the Ottoman Empire had expanded as far into Europe as Hungary, where their advance was finally halted by Holy Roman Emperor Charles V.

One of the consequences of Ottoman expansion was that a number of Greek scholars fled to Italy. They brought with them many precious manuscripts of ancient Greek classics—works that most of western Europe had previously known only in Latin translation, if at all. Western European scholars were thrilled to have access to these classics in the original language. Many Italian, Dutch, German, French, and English scholars learned to read ancient Greek. They wrote and taught about the ancient literature, translated it into their own languages, and fed the Renaissance revival of classical Greek ideas. A great number of the first printed books were Greek classics. Some scholars, notably the Dutch writer Erasmus, used their skills to study the New Testament of the Bible, which originally had been written in Greek. They made translations that were more accurate than the official Latin version of the Bible used by the Church. Such translations became very important to those who wished to reform the Church.

Ottoman expansion affected Europe in other ways, too. European rulers were very conscious of the Ottoman Empire as a threat, but they also felt a great sense of competition with the splendor of the Ottoman court. Monarchs, especially the Holy Roman Emperor, made a point of displaying their wealth in an effort to show that their states were equal in greatness to the Ottoman Empire. But in spite of the threats and rivalry, trade and other peaceful relations continued between Europe and the empire. For example, Turkish carpets were a common luxury in the homes and palaces of wealthy Europeans. And quite a few European artists, architects, and craftsmen spent time in Istanbul (as Constantinople was renamed) working for the Ottoman ruler. Historians are just beginning to thoroughly study the relationship between Renaissance Europe and the Ottoman Empire, and in the future we will probably know even more about the ways these two great civilizations influenced each other.

This portrait of Sultan Mehmed II, the conqueror of Constantinople, combines European and Turkish artistic traditions. It was painted by the great Venetian artist Gentile Bellini, who spent two years at the court of the Ottoman sultan.

RULING PASSIONS

Whether a state was governed by king, queen, duke, prince, or count, Renaissance rulers all had at least two things in common: First, they were very concerned with promoting an image of power and splendor, for if the ruler was respected and admired, so was the state as a whole. This was important in a nation's dealings with other countries and also helped uphold the ruler's authority with his or her own people. Renaissance rulers therefore pursued various means of increasing their prestige and displaying their power and wealth. For example, they surrounded themselves with luxury; supported musicians, poets, and artists; and sponsored voyages of exploration.

King Henry VIII of England radiates royal power and splendor in this portrait by his court painter, Hans Holbein the Younger.

The second common concern of Renaissance rulers was to make their authority reach all of their subjects. This was an especial challenge in large kingdoms such as England, France, and Spain. The monarch was the absolute head of state, but could not be everywhere, controlling everything. It was necessary to have a growing network of civil servants who could administer and enforce government policies across the realm.

Since the Middle Ages, rulers had had councils of noblemen and churchmen to advise them. The House of Lords of England's Parliament began as such a council, and by the Renaissance it had grown to sixty members. The English monarch was required to summon Parliament and get its approval to pass new laws or raise taxes. In England, as in many other countries, the ruler also had a smaller circle of advisers and assistants called the privy council. Its members, known as ministers or secretaries, were given responsibility for various departments of government, such as the treasury or foreign affairs.

Below the ministers and secretaries was a growing class of civil servants—officials, managers, administrators, and tax collectors charged with putting government policies into action. By about 1550 there were around 3,000 such civil servants in France, for example. At the bottom level of government was an even larger number of workers such as bookkeepers, file clerks, and copyists who took care of day-to-day details.

With so many more employees, governments became bigger, and more expensive to run. The employees needed offices to work in, too, adding new building expenses to national budgets. The Renaissance was also a time of complicated international relations, so ambassadors and spies were on government payrolls in greater numbers than ever before. Diplomacy often failed, and there was almost constant warfare throughout the period. The size of armies grew from between 12,000 and 30,000 before 1500 to around 85,000 in 1570. Armies, diplomats, office buildings, civil servants—all had to be paid for out of the ruler's own pocket. Rulers met their financial challenges by borrowing money from the great banks of the time, selling government jobs to the highest bidder—and increasing taxes. It took a truly remarkable ruler such as England's Elizabeth I to keep the devotion of her subjects even when she had to burden them with more and more taxes.

Two

PALACES AND POWER

Renaissance rulers used grand buildings and magnificent courts to help promote their image of wealth and power. In large countries such as England, France, Spain, and Sweden, monarchs had at least one palace in the nation's capital city. They also owned palaces in other parts of their realm, and sometimes moved their court from place to place.

Many rulers preferred not to live in the medieval castles of their ancestors and favored new, less fortresslike, more elegant residences. One of the most lavish palaces of the Renaissance was Chambord, built in France's Loire River valley for King Francis I between 1519 and 1547. It had 440 rooms, 365 fireplaces, 13 staircases, and stables for 1,200 horses. It was surrounded by gardens and parklands, all enclosed by a wall 22 miles in circumference. Chambord's magnificence impressed all who visited it.

There were other ways in which rulers used buildings to show their power. For example, after King Ferdinand and Queen Isabella conquered Granada, they took over the beautiful Alhambra, the palace of the king-

A portion of the royal château, or castle, of Amboise. Built during the fifteenth and sixteenth centuries, it was one of the French king's many majestic residences. Amboise is also famous as the place where Leonardo da Vinci spent his last years; he is buried in the château's chapel.

dom's former rulers. Queen Isabella moved the royal household to the Alhambra to show how completely Spain had triumphed over the Muslims. Eventually her grandson, Holy Roman Emperor Charles V, constructed a new palace right next to the Alhambra—and he made a point of having it tower over the older building.

IN THE ROYAL PRESENCE

Royal palaces in England, France, and many other countries shared common features. Just as the ruler was at the center of government, the royal apartments were at the heart of the palace. The largest, most public of these rooms was the presence chamber, or throne room. This was where the ruler gave audiences to his or her subjects, received ambassadors, heard reports from high-ranking officials, and held public ceremonies. Queen Elizabeth I's presence chamber in her palace of Hampton Court was so splendid that it was known as the Paradise Chamber. The queen's throne there was upholstered with brown velvet embroidered with gold thread and ornamented with diamonds. The Paradise Chamber also housed a collection of precious musical instruments, including two small harpsichords, one made of glass and one with strings of silver and gold.

Next there was the privy chamber, a room for smaller, more private, meetings. The privy council met with the monarch in this room. Extremely

Queen Elizabeth, attended by some of her councillors and ladies-in-waiting, receives two Dutch ambassadors in her privy chamber. Some people think this picture was painted by Low Countries artist Levina Teerlinc, who had been Henry VIII's "royal paintrix" and was a gentlewoman in Elizabeth's household.

sensitive or secret matters were often discussed with the ruler in his or her bedchamber. Its doors were well guarded, and only the most trusted advisers and attendants were allowed in. Queen Elizabeth often took her meals privately in her bedchamber, away from the great crowd of the court. But, like other rulers of the time, she was seldom left completely alone—even when she went to sleep, there were attendants who slept in her room with her.

Just outside the royal apartments there were usually rooms where servants and pages awaited orders from the ruler and the nobles of the court. There was another room where guards stood watch over the entrance to the presence chamber, turning away unwelcome visitors. The guards also made sure that those who were allowed into the presence chamber were not carrying any concealed weapons.

Royal palaces often covered many acres, with space and rooms to provide for all the court's needs. The largest room was usually a great hall, where all the court could eat meals together. The one at Hampton Court held as many as six hundred people at once. The great hall might also be the scene of plays, balls, and other entertainments. Passageways or staircases connected the great hall with the palace kitchens. Hampton Court had six kitchens, while Richmond Palace (built by Elizabeth I's grandfather) had eighteen.

Every palace had at least one chapel where members of the court could attend church services. Long galleries—wide hallways that were sometimes hundreds of feet in length—provided places for people to walk and get exercise when the weather was bad. They could also gossip or discuss political business while they strolled. Other facilities for recreation might include tilt yards where jousts were held, pits for cockfights (ladies did not attend these), and tennis courts. One of Europe's oldest existing tennis courts is at Hampton Court Palace. It was built by the order of King Henry VIII, who was very athletic as a young man and loved to play tennis.

Gardens of Earthly Delights

God Almighty first planted a garden; and indeed it is the purest of human pleasures.

—Francis Bacon (1561–1626), "On Gardens"

In Renaissance Europe, gardening became an art form. Gardens provided not only fruits, vegetables, and herbs for the table, but also gave nobles new places to express and enjoy their ideas of beauty. Gardens were carefully designed to provide picturesque views, shady arbors, and avenues of trees for strolling under. There were hedges clipped into artful shapes, colorful plantings of flowers, grassy lawns, terraces and pavilions, fountains and ponds, statues, and marble benches to rest on while enjoying all of this beauty. Some gardens featured "wilderness" areas, made to look like wild forest, and grottos, artificial cavelike structures decorated with crystals and shells. Many nobles began collecting rare and exotic plants in their gardens, and some also housed menageries, small zoos that featured wildlife from far-off lands. Naturally, such gardens were very large—Hampton Court Palace in England, for example, had sixty acres of gardens. These were safe, welcoming places to relax away from the pressures of government and court life.

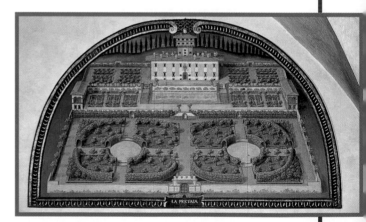

This painting shows how the large formal gardens at one of the Medici family's villas looked in 1599.

DUCAL GRANDEUR

In Italy's city-states, as in the kingdoms to the north and west, rulers displayed their wealth and power in grand palaces. They also had villas in the Italian countryside where they could go to relax, to get away from the cares of government, to escape the city's summer heat, or to enjoy the beauties of nature.

Italian nobles governed from the hearts of their cities, where they sometimes had more than one palace. For example, in the 1520s Federigo Gonzaga II of Mantua had a lavish new palace built for himself on the edge of the city. Called the Palazzo del Te, it was within walking distance of the

A group portrait of the Gonzaga family, rulers of Mantua, with some of their courtiers and servants. This fresco, one of many that decorated the walls of Mantua's ducal palace, was painted around 1470 by the great Andrea Mantegna, who was court artist to the Gonzaga family for more than forty years.

ducal palace where Federigo conducted government business. The new palace was a retreat where he could enjoy himself and entertain friends and guests. One of his first guests at the Palazzo del Te was Emperor Charles V. The emperor was so impressed by Federigo's display of wealth and importance that he raised him from the rank of marquis to duke.

Italian palaces did not follow a set pattern. The dukes of Milan ruled from the city's medieval castle-fortress. In contrast, the duke of Urbino's residence, built during the 1470s, was "more like a city than a mere palace," according to a prominent writer of the time. This large and imposing palace was constructed in the center of Urbino. It was a complex of a number of connected buildings arranged around three spacious courtyards. The duke's pride was his *studiolo*, a sumptuously painted room that was devoted to his huge collection of books.

The Medici palace in Florence, completed in the 1450s, also drew comments on its grandeur—one writer remarked that it was "a palace that throws even the Colosseum at Rome into the shade." Iron gates led from the street into the inner courtyard of the massive stone building. On the ground floor were offices for the family's merchant and banking business, a banquet hall, and a chapel, with a floor of inlaid marble and walls painted with frescoes by one of Florence's leading artists. The next floor had a large reception room where city officials, citizens, ambassadors from other cities, and the like could meet with the head of the Medici family. Other rooms on the palace's upper floors included bedrooms for as many as fifty people, including servants and guests as well as the family. The privileged members of the household could stroll around a loggia, or covered balcony, that looked out over the main courtyard. Visitors were often taken to the *studiolo* to admire the Medicis' collection of books and precious gems. But it was the palace's everyday conveniences that most impressed one visiting writer. After describing all the kitchens, pantries, storerooms, wells, and latrines, he remarked with approval that the builder had "not left out anything that is convenient."

Three

COURTLY
COMMUNITIES

A Renaissance court had two important, overlapping roles. First, it was the household of the ruler. The household included all sorts of servants and officials to take care of the ruler's, and his or her family's, needs. There were guards, personal attendants, secretaries, and bookkeepers; cooks, waiters, and entertainers. Horses, dogs, and falcons used for hunting—a favorite sport—had to be cared for. Palaces needed to be cleaned and kept in good repair, and gardens had to be tended. It took a huge number of people to meet all these needs—for example, about 800 in the small court of the duke of Mantua, and nearly 2,000 in the court of the French king.

In addition to being the greatest household in the state, the court was also the seat of government. Day-to-day administrative tasks might be carried out in buildings designed for that use alone. But actual government decisions were made in the ruler's palace itself, where the ruler consulted with heads of departments and other leading members of the court.

A Noble Household

A Renaissance court was a household made up of government officials, advisers, servants, visiting ambassadors, family members, churchmen, entertainers, and others. At the center of the court, of course, was the ruler. When the ruler traveled—for instance, from a city palace to a villa or hunting lodge in the countryside—much of the court went along.

The household of Duke Galeazzo Maria Sforza of Milan provides a good example of the number and kinds of people who could be found at court. The duke's "inner household" included four "best friends," valets, footmen, pageboys, and other personal servants. The duchess also had an array of attendants, including gentlemen, lady companions, chambermaids, and her old nurse. The ducal children were served by governesses, tutors, wet nurses, and others. Many of the duke's relatives—brothers, sisters, aunts, uncles, and cousins—also lived at court, along with their servants and attendants.

There were a number of specialized servants in the duke's household: an apothecary, a perfume maker, a surgeon, and physicians; tailors, shoemakers, huntsmen, and kennel keepers; tennis players, trumpet players, and jesters. An official called the Master of Works oversaw the artists and engineers employed by the duke. The Master of Stables oversaw the grooms and others who took care of the horses. Seneschals were in charge of the servants responsible for the cleaning and upkeep of the duke's various homes. Stewards supervised the many kitchen workers and dining servants. The duke's household also included priests, along with singers and musicians to provide music for religious services.

Among the government personnel at Duke Galeazzo Maria's court were the members of his privy council and council of justice, diplomats, chancellors, tax officials, judges, administrators, and secretaries. There were a number of gentlemen courtiers who could be assigned various tasks and missions as needed. Ambassadors and dignitaries from other states also lived at or visited the

duke's court. Then there were all the military personnel who served the duke: the Commissioner of Armed Forces, the army commanders, the ducal guards, the messengers, and others.

A royal or noble household had a large staff, which included guards and soldiers such as this young man, who is armed with both a sword and a halberd, a staff with a metal pike on its end.

COUNCILLORS AND FAVOR SEEKERS

The most important members of a royal court were the privy council. Some rulers relied on this council more than others. Even in a single country, the number of councillors and the frequency of their meetings could vary. In England, for example, Queen Mary I had as many as sixty privy councillors. Her sister and successor, Elizabeth I, had only thirteen to fifteen men on her council. At first she met with them three times a week, but by the end of her reign she was meeting with the council every day.

William Cecil, Lord Burghley, Queen Elizabeth's most trusted adviser. He shared the queen's love of learning, and the two often discussed classical literature as well as affairs of state.

A man could serve as a trusted adviser on such a council without being nobly born. Elizabeth's principal secretary, the councillor she depended on most, was William Cecil, a gentleman lawyer. Eventually Elizabeth raised him to the noble rank of baron and gave him the post of Lord Treasurer of England. The possibility of this kind of advancement drew many gentlemen to royal and noble courts.

Rulers had the power to give out all sorts of honors, offices, promotions, commissions, and favors. The greatest noblemen, with extensive lands and lavish residences of their own, often lived at their monarch's court for at least part of the year. Whether or not they received any important appointment or great favor from the ruler, just being at court added a certain distinction and brilliance to their reputations. There were always numerous men of lesser rank—gentlemen, knights, and younger sons of the nobility—at court hoping for recognition, seeking government posts, or looking for ways to advance their careers. The charming Robert Dudley was a courtier of this kind. He was Elizabeth I's Master of the Horse, in charge of the royal stables. He delighted the queen with his wit, his liveliness, and his skills in horsemanship, jousting, dancing, and languages. She singled him out as a favorite and eventually made him earl of Leicester.

Some favor seekers had serious projects in mind. When Christopher Columbus, of Genoa, Italy, wanted to find a route to Asia by sailing westward across the Atlantic, he went first to the king of Portugal for support. The Portuguese, however, were already spending their money on explorations around the coast of Africa. Columbus went next to the king and queen of Spain. Ferdinand and Isabella kept Columbus in their service for five years before they finally decided to fund his voyage. Other rulers also welcomed explorers to their courts. For example, Elizabeth I gave a knighthood to Francis Drake after he successfully sailed all the way around the earth.

COURTING CREATIVITY

Many writers came to court hoping to find royal or noble patrons. Even though the printing press made it possible to get books into the hands of more people than ever before, most authors earned little or nothing from the sales of their books. Instead, writers often dedicated their works—in

Singing and playing a musical instrument were recommended accomplishments for ladies. Although most courts generally had a staff of professional singers and musicians, music was a popular pastime for many noble women and men. These three ladies seem to be concentrating hard on learning a new song together. Later, perhaps, they may perform the piece for a group of their friends.

words of glowing praise—to wealthy, distinguished, influential individuals. The recipients of these dedications often returned the compliment by giving writers gifts of money or assistance with their careers.

Some Renaissance rulers sought out writers to be part of their court. Writers could provide poems and plays to entertain the court, histories to glorify the great deeds of the ruler's family and the state, translations and studies of ancient classics, or books of advice and guidance. Baldassare Castiglione lived at the courts of Milan, Mantua, and Urbino, where he wrote *The Courtier,* one of the Renaissance's most famous and popular works of literature. In it he described the ideal accomplishments, qualities, and behavior for men and women at court. Many writers at court also served as teachers for the ruler's children, or they might take on duties such as private secretary or royal ambassador. Thomas More, a gifted scholar as well as the author of *Utopia* (a book that described an imaginary place with a perfect society) and other works, belonged to the court of Henry VIII. Henry gave More a number of government posts, a knighthood, and eventually made him Lord Chancellor of England. On the other hand, the renowned Dutch writer and scholar Erasmus turned down generous invitations to live at the courts of the duke of Bavaria and the kings of England, France, and Spain, preferring to be free to go where he pleased.

Musicians, singers, and composers were also part of court life, providing music for entertainment, processions, celebrations, dancing, and church services. They also might give music lessons to both children and adults at court, because the ideal nobleman or lady was expected to be skilled at singing or playing an instrument. Nearly every court employed musicians, sometimes dozens of them. The courts of the dukes of Burgundy, the dukes of Ferrara, the kings of France, and the Holy Roman Emperors were especially notable as thriving centers of music where the greatest composers lived and worked.

A Genius
and His Patrons

Think of the great figures of the Renaissance, and one of the first people who comes to mind is probably Leonardo da Vinci. Artist, architect, inventor, engineer—Leonardo was all these and more. His genius was well known in his own lifetime, and his talents were sought after by princely patrons.

Leonardo began his career in Florence, where his paintings were admired by Lorenzo de' Medici. In 1482, when Leonardo was thirty years old, Lorenzo sent him as a kind of goodwill ambassador to the court of Ludovico Sforza in Milan. Ludovico was an intelligent, cultured, talented man who enjoyed being surrounded by artists and scholars. He was also ambitious and eager to glorify his family. Leonardo's first job in Milan was to create a huge bronze statue of Ludovico's father astride a rearing horse.

The statue never became a reality because of technical problems, but the designs for it were impressive. Ludovico was happy to have Leonardo working on other projects for him, and the artist exercised his talents for architecture, engineering, and urban planning. Leonardo designed everything from military machinery to a new sewer system to suburban street layouts. Ludovico used some of these ideas, while others remained only plans in Leonardo's notebooks full of sketches and diagrams.

Leonardo was popular at court. He designed new houses for many of Ludovico's courtiers. The artist also played a key role in Milan's courtly entertainments, for which he created stage sets, elaborate costumes, and special effects. Still, Ludovico was often frustrated by his favorite artist, who had difficulty focusing on one thing at a time and often took far too long to complete projects.

For his part, Leonardo did not get paid by the court on a regular basis, so he had to take on jobs for other clients as well. In addition, he had a great variety of interests that he wanted to explore. He studied anatomy so that his por-

trayals of the human body in motion would be more realistic. He was fascinated by geometry and drew illustrations for a mathematics book by his friend Luca Pacioli, who also lived at court. His curiosity about the world around him and his inventive imagination were expressed in sketch after sketch in his notebooks.

In 1499 King Louis XII of France conquered Milan. Ludovico Sforza escaped to Germany, and Leonardo was forced to go in search of new patrons. He spent short periods in Mantua, at the court of Isabella d'Este, and in Venice, where he drew up some defense plans for the city. While in Venice he also designed a bridge for the sultan of the Ottoman Empire. Moving on, he revisited Florence, then briefly entered the service of Cesare Borgia, the son of the pope. In 1503 Leonardo returned to Florence, where he was welcomed and honored.

Three years later, Leonardo went back to Milan. The city-state was still under French rule, but it was a good home for artists and scholars all the same. Leonardo trained apprentices; studied perspective, optics, and ballooning (among many other subjects, of course); and became absorbed by various engineering projects. He devised a system of locks that controlled water levels in a canal, enabling boats to navigate the canal for the first time. Leonardo's invention of locks was a great contribution to boating and shipping, and it also had immediate rewards for the inventor: Louis XII gave Leonardo a regular salary.

In 1511 the French were driven out of Milan—and so was Leonardo, since he had served the French. After two years of living quietly in a friend's home, he set out for Rome, where Giovanni de' Medici (Lorenzo's son) had just become Pope Leo X. The new pope gave Leonardo various engineering assignments, such as draining a marsh. In his spare time, Leonardo pursued his other interests, designing machines and costumes, studying ancient Roman culture and mythology, creating geometrical puzzles, and so on.

In 1516 Francis I, recently come to the French throne, persuaded Leonardo to join his court. Francis gave the artist a luxurious home, a generous yearly salary, and the title Painter, Engineer, and Architect of the Realm. Francis required little work from the artist, whose health was failing, but simply took pride in having such a renowned man at his court. Thanks to the French king, Leonardo was able to spend the last few years of his life in comfort, security, and honor.

Leonardo da Vinci's Portrait of a Lady with an Ermine, *painted while he was Ludovico Sforza's court artist in Milan. The young woman so masterfully portrayed was Cecilia Gallerani, Ludovico's favorite among the ladies of his court.*

The Renaissance love of music was international, and many musicians, singers, and composers worked at courts far from the lands of their birth. Artists, too, were much sought after, and many traveled away from home in pursuit of their careers. For example, Sofonisba Anguissola (one of Europe's first famous women painters), from a noble family of Cremona, Italy, spent time in the Spanish court, teaching the queen to paint. King Henry VIII's court painter was Hans Holbein the Younger, a German who worked in Switzerland before coming to England. Venice's greatest artist, Titian, stayed at the Holy Roman Emperor's court in Augsburg, Germany, on several occasions. The renowned Leonardo da Vinci spent time at several different courts. On the other hand, numerous artists were able to find work closer to home, especially in Italy. As a young man, the painter and sculptor Michelangelo, son of a respectable Florence family, lived in the Medici palace (also home to a collection of noted philosophers and writers). The duke of Urbino's court included several artists and architects. Among them was Raphael, who spent his childhood at this court and grew up to become one of the Renaissance's greatest painters.

four

COURTIERS AND PRINCES

Educated people in the Renaissance—including many in the ruling class—tended to be very interested in philosophical explanations of life. One of the ancient writers rediscovered by the Renaissance was the Greek philosopher Plato. During the Middle Ages, only one of his books was known to most Europeans. But during the second half of the fifteenth century, Cosimo de' Medici commissioned the scholar Marsilio Ficino to translate the complete works of Plato from Greek into Latin. At this time Latin was understood by most educated Europeans, and so Plato's writings finally became widely available. Another ancient philosopher who had great influence was Aristotle, whose works had been taught in European universities since the 1200s.

Plato, in his theory of forms, described everything in the world as an imperfect reflection of that thing's true form, which exists in the unseen world of ideas. Renaissance writers in turn sought to describe the ideal forms of everything from beauty to religion. Plato himself had written about the ideal commonwealth, concluding that it should be ruled by a king who was also a philosopher. Aristotle's influential writings on ethics and politics described ideals of behavior. To live a good life, he recommended that people practice the virtues of steadfastness, moderation, justice, and common sense, as well as generosity, magnificence, ambition, friendliness, truthfulness, wit, and self-esteem balanced by humility. The philosophies of Plato and Aristotle came together in Renaissance writings that described the ideal nobleman or ruler.

Two of the most important books of the Renaissance were *The Courtier* by Baldassare Castiglione and *The Prince* by Niccolò Machiavelli. Each author, in his own way, described what he thought it took to succeed in various aspects of court life. Castiglione's ideal courtier and Machiavelli's ideal ruler were quite different from each other. But by looking at them, we can begin to get a sense of what the life of a Renaissance courtier or king was like.

THE IDEAL NOBLEMAN

The Courtier, published in 1528, became incredibly popular all over Renaissance Europe—by 1600 more than a hundred editions, in several languages, had been produced. Castiglione was influenced not only by Plato and Aristotle but also by the Roman writer Cicero's *On Duties*. Renaissance scholars looked to this book as the major ancient resource for how to conduct oneself in a fitting and dignified manner. *The Courtier* in turn was recognized everywhere in Europe as the definitive modern guidebook for gentlemanly behavior. The book emphasized that everything in life could be made a work of art—a true Renaissance philosophy.

Castiglione believed that a courtier's purpose in life was to influence his ruler to govern wisely, like the ideal philosopher-king described by

Baldassare Castiglione's The Courtier *was one of the most popular and influential books written during the Renaissance. This painting of Castiglione is by Raphael and is widely regarded as one of the great artist's finest portraits.*

Plato. In order to exert this influence, the courtier first had to get the ruler's attention, and then had to make sure that his company continued to please the ruler. Castiglione recommended that courtiers have the virtues and accomplishments that would best meet these goals.

The perfect courtier was a gentleman from a good family. He was handsome, intelligent, witty, and tactful. He was athletic, a skilled soldier and rider—if there was no battle to fight, he could demonstrate these qualities in jousts, hunting, tennis, and swimming. He ought to know at least two languages besides his own. Dancing, music, poetry, and painting were arts that he should cultivate, or at least be able to appreciate. And he should distinguish himself in all this with grace and no apparent effort.

Once a courtier had his ruler's attention and favor, he should remain humble and not get greedy. He should not try to increase his influence by speaking evil of other courtiers, and he should never pressure the ruler for promotions for himself or his friends. Instead, it was best for him to let his actions speak for themselves and to wait patiently for the ruler to reward his services. Castiglione concluded that "to purchase favor at great men's hands, there is no better way than to deserve it."

Did *The Courtier* have any relationship to the lives of real men who lived at Europe's courts? Castiglione himself was a courtier, and his writing portrayed an ideal that was based on what he observed—many courtiers throughout Europe did indeed have at least some of the qualities he described. At Elizabeth I's court in England, for example, there was Sir Walter Raleigh. Handsome, learned, and witty, Raleigh was a successful sea captain, explorer, and soldier. He wrote poetry; dressed in the height of fashion; discussed philosophy, mathematics, and other advanced subjects; and conducted scientific experiments. He was a perfect example of what has come to be known as the Renaissance Man, an achiever in many areas of life. There were numerous others like him. Still, even with the influence of the most accomplished courtiers, very few rulers became ideal philosopher-kings.

COURTIERS AND PRINCES · 39

Princely Poetry

In his youth, King Henry VIII of England was widely regarded as a model of royal manhood. Handsome, fashionable, athletic, enthusiastic about both warfare and the arts, he also enjoyed writing poems and songs. Here is one of his songs, which celebrates a love that is as enduring as the greenness of holly and ivy leaves, which keep their color even in the winter.

Green groweth the holly,
So doth the ivy.
Though winter blasts blow never so high,
Green groweth the holly.

As the holly groweth green,
And never changeth hue,
So I am, ever hath been,
Unto my lady true.

As the holly groweth green
With ivy all alone
When flowers cannot be seen
And greenwood leaves be gone,

Now unto my lady,
Promise to her I make
From all other only
To her I me betake.

Adieu, mine own lady,
Adieu, my special,

Who hath my heart truly,
Be sure, and ever shall.

Green groweth the holly,
So doth the ivy.
Though winter blasts blow never so high,
Green groweth the holly.

This portrait of Henry VIII was painted when the king was about forty-five years old.

RULING IN THE REAL WORLD

Niccolò Machiavelli's *The Prince*, published in 1532, was almost as well known as *The Courtier*, but it did not earn the same admiration. It dealt with the problems of ruling a state in a way that many people found too ruthlessly realistic for comfort. Machiavelli saw that there was a large gap between how a man ought to live and how he actually did live. It was desirable to follow the traditional virtues described by Aristotle and others, but a ruler had to be prepared to be unvirtuous when necessary. For example, even though the ideal prince would always be honest and keep his word, sometimes in real life telling a lie—or at least not admitting to the truth— was far better than risking the security of the state.

A ruler, wrote Machiavelli, ought to be manly, brave, serious, and decisive. He needed to stay in shape, to always be fit for battle. He should appear to be virtuous but should be as cunning as a fox and as mighty as a lion. So long as he had the goodwill of his people, he could indulge in virtues such as justice and mercy. But sometimes—especially when dealing with newly conquered territory—he was better off to have a reputation for cruelty. Nevertheless, he should only be feared, not hated.

The prince should avoid flatterers but at the same time should not allow those around him to undermine his authority by voicing their opinions too strongly. Therefore, he needed to choose wise men as his councillors or ministers, and not allow them to give him advice until he asked for it. Then he ought to follow their good advice and reward them generously to keep their loyalty.

Machiavelli recommended that a ruler study history to learn from the successes and failures of great leaders of the past. It was also wise to patronize men of talent and to support business and agriculture in his realm. He should sponsor festivities and entertainments for his people, and give them an example of courtesy and benevolence—so long as none of this undermined his dignity and the people's respect for him.

Machiavelli was a government official in Florence, and he wrote largely from his experiences of the ups and downs of his city. He also used real-life examples of European rulers. For instance, Emperor Maximilian I was a poor ruler because he was secretive, frequently changed his mind, and did not follow the good advice of his councillors. Cesare Borgia, who conquered much of central Italy on behalf of the pope, and Isabella and Ferdinand of Spain were successful rulers because they extended their realms with ruthless single-mindedness and cunning.

THE BUSINESS OF WAR

Machiavelli wrote that a prince should devote great energy to the skills of warfare, which were of the greatest importance to both extend and defend his state. This was advice that many rulers definitely agreed with. Sometimes rulers planned military campaigns from their palaces, or authorized others to head their armies for them. Sometimes a ruler led his troops in person. This could spell disaster, for he might be killed—like King Ludwig II of Bohemia and Hungary, who fell in battle against the Ottoman Turks—or taken prisoner. Francis I of France, fighting Emperor Charles V for territory in northern Italy, was captured and imprisoned for a year. He was also forced to leave his sons in Spain as hostages, and to gain their freedom he had to pay Charles a ransom that equalled more than three and a half tons of gold—a huge drain on France's treasury.

Just as such defeats could humiliate a ruler, victory added considerably to a leader's glory. Charles V had vast resources and could put huge numbers of men and weapons on the field. With his brother Ferdinand (who became king of Bohemia and Hungary after King Ludwig's death), he stopped an Ottoman invasion of Austria and drove the Turks back to eastern Hungary. A few years later he successfully attacked Tunis, in North Africa, the headquarters of Ottoman pirates who had been threatening

This design for one of The Conquest of Tunis *tapestries shows a horse being lowered into a boat during the course of a battle. The artist, Jan Vermeyen, was an eyewitness to the scene, for Charles V had hired him to travel with the army and make drawings recording the military campaign.*

trade in the Mediterranean. Even though the piracy soon resumed, Charles's action had great symbolic importance as a victory of Christians over a Muslim superpower. Charles ordered twelve tapestries—the most expensive and luxurious form of art—made to commemorate the battle. *The Conquest of Tunis* tapestries were afterward displayed on several occasions when Charles wished to emphasize the power of his family and empire.

The noblemen who ruled Italy's city-states also spent much of their time, energy, and money on warfare. Some fought to conquer new territory for their states, while others were forced to fight to defend them—sometimes against the vastly superior forces of France or the Holy Roman Empire. Some

Italian noblemen were professional soldiers who hired themselves out as generals to lead the armies of other states. Federigo da Montefeltro, who became duke of Urbino in 1474, was the most successful noble mercenary of his time. His earnings as a general made him fabulously wealthy. He used his riches to patronize artists, to beautify his palace, and to build a huge and magnificent book collection that was admired all over Italy. In this way he turned his prowess as a warrior into a reputation as a generous patron and a nobleman of cultured taste, refinement, and learning.

five

LADIES IN A MAN'S WORLD

In many ways, the Renaissance court was a man's world. Women had almost no official role to play in government. Many, however, were able to exercise power unofficially, temporarily, or behind the scenes—usually because circumstances forced them to do so. For example, Isabella d'Este governed the city-state of Mantua during the ten-year illness of her husband, Marquis Francesco Gonzaga II. After Caterina Sforza's husband was killed, she took over his command of the defense of the Italian city of Forli against a besieging army.

Sometimes a ruler came to rely on a female relative to help him govern. Emperor Charles V made his sister, Maria of Hungary, his regent over the Low Countries. King Henry II of France depended heavily on his wife, Catherine de' Medici. When he went to war, he appointed her regent of France and entrusted her with supplying his army. He afterward made a habit of seeking her advice on government matters, especially foreign rela-

At most courts there were fewer women than men, but a queen or high-ranking noblewoman always had ladies to attend her and women servants to wait on her. This fresco of two noble attendants and a servant was painted by Paolo Uccello in 1440.

tions. When Henry died, Catherine governed the nation on behalf of their young sons for many years.

A few Renaissance women did have the lawful right to rule. Mary of Burgundy was duchess in her own right, although her husband Maximilian (later Holy Roman Emperor) governed Burgundy for her. Queen Isabella inherited the throne of Castile in Spain; she ruled jointly with her husband Ferdinand of Aragon and in many ways was the more powerful of the two. Then there were Mary I and Elizabeth I of England, and Mary Queen of Scots. All three inherited the crown because their royal fathers had no living sons to rule instead. Mary I ruled for only five years, and made herself unpopular with the English people by persecuting Protestants and by marrying King Philip II of Spain. Mary of Scotland became queen when she was a baby, but from the ages of five to nineteen she lived at the French court. For four of those years she was married to the king of France (Catherine de' Medici's oldest son). She only returned to Scotland after his death in 1560. A few years later she remarried and had a son. She was never popular with her people and was always in conflict with the Scottish nobles. In 1567 she was forced to pass the crown on to her child.

Of the Renaissance's women rulers, only Elizabeth I was able to successfully govern her realm on her own. One reason she was able to manage this was that she refused to marry. "I am married to England," she once proclaimed. Elizabeth knew that if she took a husband, she would then be queen in name only. Almost everyone in Renaissance Europe believed that a wife must give way to her husband in all decisions—whether those decisions applied to running a household or to governing a kingdom.

SUPPORTING THE ARTS

Even if noble and royal women rarely had the opportunity to govern, they could still play an important role as patrons of learning and the arts. For

Queen Elizabeth's Speech to Her Army

In 1588 a Spanish fleet, the Armada, set sail to invade England. In this national emergency, Queen Elizabeth I went in person to rally the troops gathering to fight the coming invasion. As Elizabeth says at the beginning of her speech, some of her councillors were afraid that this public appearance would expose her to danger. But the queen believed it was important to set an example of courage for her army.

My loving people,

We have been persuaded by some that are careful of our safety, to take heed how we commit our selves to armed multitudes, for fear of treachery; but I assure you I do not desire to live to distrust my faithful and loving people. . . . I have always so behaved myself that, under God, I have placed my chiefest strength and safeguard in the loyal hearts and good-will of my subjects; and therefore I am come amongst you . . . not for my recreation and disport, but being resolved, in the midst and heat of the battle, to live or die amongst you all; to lay down for my God, and for my kingdom, and my people, my honour and my blood, even in the dust. I know I have the body but of a weak and feeble woman; but I have the heart and stomach of a king, and of a king of England too, and think foul to scorn that . . . Spain, or any prince of Europe, should dare to invade the borders of my realm; to which rather than any dishonour shall grow by me, I myself will take up arms, I myself will be your general, judge, and rewarder of every one of your virtues in the field. . . . In the meantime, my lieutenant general shall be in my stead, than whom never prince commanded a more noble or worthy subject; not doubting but by your obedience to my general, by your concord in the camp, and your valour in the field, we shall shortly have a famous victory over those enemies of my God, of my kingdom, and of my people.

example, Catherine of Aragon, Henry VIII's first wife, supported Erasmus and other scholar-writers. Marguerite of Austria, Duchess of Burgundy, patronized some of the best composers, singers, and musicians of northern Europe. Anne of Brittany, married to a king of France, ordered French translations of books by distinguished Italian authors and invited other educated women to court to discuss philosophy with her.

The most enthusiastic of all Renaissance patrons of the arts was probably Isabella d'Este. At her husband's court in Mantua, she surrounded herself with beautifully crafted luxuries: engraved jewels; vases and cups carved from semiprecious stones; inlaid boxes; gold, silver, and bronze medallions; custom-painted playing cards; and musical instruments. A talented musician and singer herself, she employed composers and numerous musicians to provide the court with music for all occasions. She decorated her *studiolo* with ancient statues and also commissioned paintings from some of the best Italian artists of her own time. Books were another passion of hers, and she had a large library; many of the books were produced specifically for her. She exchanged witty, intelligent letters with artists, musicians, and poets and was famous throughout Italy for her learning and her devotion to collecting both ancient and modern artworks.

Duchess Isabetta Gonzaga often brought together writers and thinkers at her court in Urbino, and Castiglione used such a gathering as the setting for *The Courtier*. In the book, Isabetta and her guests discuss not only the ideal courtier but also the ideal court lady. All agree that she should be beautiful, charming, intelligent, witty, well mannered, sweet, and virtuous. She also ought to be good at music, dancing, conversation, and playing games such as chess. Some of the duchess's guests feel that these accomplishments, along with the ability to manage a household wisely, are all that ladies need. But one guest, Giuliano de' Medici, insists "you will find that worth has constantly prevailed among women as among men; and that there have always been women who have undertaken wars and won glorious victories, governed kingdoms with the greatest prudence and jus-

This lady was probably a member of the court of Queen Isabella of Spain. The artist portrayed her with the quiet modesty that many people thought was one of the most important characteristics of the ideal lady.

tice, and done all that men have done. As for the sciences [meaning various branches of knowledge], do you not remember reading of many women who were learned in philosophy? Others who excelled in poetry? Others who prosecuted, accused and defended before judges with great eloquence? As for manual works [things made with the hands, such as arts and crafts], it would be too long to tell of them."

Queen for a Day

Elizabeth I was a busy monarch. On a typical day she rose early and probably breakfasted in her chamber. After eating she used toothpicks and soft cloths to clean her teeth. She might also sweeten her breath with rosemary or cinnamon and perfume herself with rosewater.

When it was time to get dressed, the queen was assisted by her ladies-in-waiting and maids of honor. This process could be lengthy, especially if the queen was preparing for any kind of ceremony. She had hundreds of gowns to choose from and, like other upper-class women of the time, dressed in several layers of clothing. Then there were the long strands of pearls, the rings, and other jewelry to put on. If it was a business-as-usual day, however, the queen preferred to dress more simply, though still elegantly.

For morning exercise, Elizabeth generally danced six or seven galliards. She liked to exercise in private so that she could feel free to dance the men's galliard steps, which were livelier than the women's. She might also give some time in the morning to singing and playing music. Then she got down to the business of government. A great deal of the queen's day was devoted to reading and answering letters, meeting with her advisers, deciding what matters to bring to her council, and other affairs of state.

In the afternoon Elizabeth liked to walk in one of her gardens, or in a gallery of the palace if the weather was unpleasant. Her favorite companions on these walks were scholars with whom she could enjoy learned conversation. After this she often rode out in her coach so that she could be among her people. Sometimes, if there were no pressing matters for her to attend to, she would spend this time hunting with hounds or falcons, accompanied by many courtiers.

The evening was a time for banqueting, dancing, and entertainments. Elizabeth did not care for large, heavy meals but enjoyed poultry, fine white bread, and light beer. She often preferred to dine privately in her chamber. But there was little real privacy for the queen. Some of her ladies-in-waiting and maids of honor

were nearly always with her. These companions and attendants were noblewomen or gentlewomen, some of them related to the queen on her mother's side. They attended to all her personal needs, even emptying her chamber pots. Maids of honor slept in her bedchamber, too. (Ladies-in-waiting, who were married women, generally attended the queen only during the daytime.)

Of course the maids of honor had no privacy, either. Many of them came to court in search of a husband—but they had better be sure they had the queen's permission before they got married! Elizabeth kept a close eye on these young women. Keeping them from getting involved with unsuitable men was just one more item on the busy monarch's daily to-do list.

Queen Elizabeth, with ladies-in-waiting and courtiers, holds court in this scene painted by a twentieth-century artist. Elizabeth has remained one of the world's most admired rulers right up to the present day.

The courtly environment gave many women various opportunities to exercise their intelligence and creativity. Marguerite of Navarre, sister of the king of France, not only patronized scholars and writers but also wrote notable books of her own. Mary Sidney Herbert, Countess of Pembroke, was one of Elizabeth I's ladies-in-waiting, like her mother before her. Many learned men and authors, including her brother, the poet and courtier Sir Philip Sidney, gathered at her magnificent country home. The countess wrote beautiful poetry, edited and published her brother's poems, and translated the Psalms and other works into English. Queen Elizabeth herself was an accomplished poet as well as a devoted supporter of writers and scholars.

HAPPILY EVER AFTER?

During the Renaissance, nearly all women were expected to marry and have children. This was especially true in Europe's ruling families. Marriage was used as a tool to strengthen political ties between states and as a means of increasing a family's wealth and reputation. Once married, a wife's most important task was to give birth to sons who could inherit their father's rank and lands.

Catherine de' Medici's story provides an example of what marriage and motherhood could be like for Renaissance noblewomen. Catherine belonged to Florence's great ruling family, but she became an orphan at the age of three. When she was twelve, her distant cousin Pope Clement VII arranged for her to marry Henry, son of the king of France. Usually it was important for a noble bride to bring a large dowry of money or property to her marriage. Circumstances had left Catherine poor, but the French king agreed to the marriage to win the favor of the pope.

Catherine and Henry married when they were both fourteen. According to custom, the pope and the king of France each visited the young couple's bedroom on the wedding night to make sure that the marriage was starting off properly. But for a long time, Catherine was unable to get pregnant. Her failure to provide a son for the heir to the French throne turned most of the court against her. Some people even believed that she must be an evil, unnatural woman, and leading courtiers recommended that Henry divorce her. Like other women in similar situations, Catherine sought the help of astrologers and magicians as well as doctors and priests, but without success.

After eleven years of marriage, Catherine at last gave birth to a son. She had nine more babies over the next decade. Even so, her husband cared little for her till late in his life. Henry's great love was another woman at court, Diane of Poitiers. The resourceful Catherine, however, managed to make friends with Diane, and she was also friendly with the king and his brilliant sister, Marguerite of Navarre. Eventually Henry, too, came to regard Catherine with affection and respect, and their last years of marriage were happy ones.

Catherine de' Medici was the mother of three kings of France, who all relied heavily on her advice. Catherine also had a strong influence on the arts and other aspects of culture—for example, introducing Italian dancing and cooking to the French court.

CHILDHOOD AT COURT

ven among royalty and nobility, childbirth was difficult and dangerous. Medical knowledge was advancing, but doctors and midwives still had few techniques to help out if something went wrong during birth. No one knew about germs, so no measures were taken to prevent infections, and there were no antibiotics to treat them. Children born alive and healthy were still vulnerable to the plagues and other diseases that were common during the Renaissance. Many families, even in the nobility, saw nearly half their children die before the age of twenty.

EARLY YEARS

The birth of a healthy child—especially a son—was greeted with great rejoicing, often celebrated with a magnificent feast. In Catholic and most Protestant families, the baby was taken to church within a few days of birth

This painting by Venice's Giovanni Bellini shows a baby wrapped in swaddling bands. Swaddling helped babies stay warm and feel secure, but the bands were usually so tight that the babies could not move their arms or legs.

to be baptized. (Some Protestants, though, did not believe in baptizing infants.) This ceremony welcomed the child into the Christian community.

Renaissance babies spent most of their time tightly swaddled in cloth bands. Otherwise, it was thought, their arms and legs might become malformed. They were rocked in their cradles, bathed, fed, and otherwise cared for mostly by servants. The most important of these servants was the nurse. Her main job was to breastfeed the baby, which she usually did until he or she was two to three years of age.* Even though the nurse was a ser-

*Noblewomen usually did not breastfeed their children, even though doctors, priests, and scholars published many writings that urged them to do so. These authors recognized the emotional and health benefits of mothers nursing their infants. But most Europeans held a long-standing belief that if a nursing mother became pregnant, her milk could poison the baby she was breastfeeding. Noblewomen were expected to bear as many children as possible, so their frequent pregnancies prevented them from being able to nurse their own babies, according to the beliefs of the time.

vant, real closeness and affection often grew between her and the child she took care of. This was especially true if the child was female. As a noble girl grew up, her nurse often continued to be her companion, attendant, and friend, sometimes even accompanying her to her husband's home when she married.

Up to about the age of seven, mothers were generally in charge of their children's upbringing, giving the first lessons in religion, values, manners, and sometimes reading and writing. During this phase of childhood, boys and girls tended to be treated somewhat alike. They even dressed similarly, in long gowns. But at six or seven, a boy was given his first pair of breeches. In England this occasion was called "breeching," and the family gave a party to celebrate. Now boys and girls began to prepare for their adult roles in earnest.

LEARNING TO BE NOBLE

Noble families—in particular, fathers—made plans for their children's futures early. Marriages were sometimes arranged before the future bride and groom were even ten years old. A girl might then be sent to live with and be educated in the family of her husband-to-be; this happened to Mary Queen of Scots when she was five years old. In Catholic families, plans were often made for a younger son to become a priest or monk, or for a daughter to become a nun. In this case, around the age of seven the child would probably enter a monastery or convent to be educated for the religious life.

For the most part, royal and noble children were educated at home. Since most girls were not expected to play any role in government or public life, their studies were often limited to a little bit of reading and a lot of spinning, sewing, embroidery, manners, and morals. Their main teachers in these and other household matters were usually their mothers and nurses. These girls might also receive lessons from music and dance teachers.

Some noble girls were lucky enough to receive the same kind of instruction as the boys of their social class. During the Renaissance, this education was more and more often a humanist one. Humanist scholars and teachers recommended a course of study using ancient Greek and Roman texts and based on ancient models of education. The main subjects were those known as the humanities: grammar (or languages), literature, history, philosophy, and rhetoric (the art of persuasive writing and public speaking). Humanists believed that studying the humanities involved students' characters as well as their minds, giving them the best preparation to fully participate in society. But even girls who received a humanist education usually did not learn rhetoric, since this was an art that Renaissance women were rarely allowed to practice.

The School of Princes

In 1423 Gianfrancesco Gonzaga I began an educational revolution. He invited the humanist scholar Vittorino da Feltre to his court in Mantua and asked him to educate the Gonzaga children—daughters as well as sons. Vittorino taught in a new way, emphasizing learning by doing more than memorization and repetition. Like other humanists, he believed that education should develop the whole person—mind, spirit, character, and body—and that it was of utmost importance for students to learn how to think for themselves. Vittorino's lessons in Greek and Latin, mathematics, music, art, religion, history, poetry, and philosophy were so enjoyable that his school was known as Casa Giocosa, "Merry House." It soon became famous all over Italy, and noble children from other cities came to Mantua to study with Vittorino. In fact, so many young nobles were educated at Casa Giocosa that it also came to be called the School of Princes.

A boy concentrates on his geometry lesson, benefiting from the hands-on learning offered by his teacher.

In addition to the humanities, it was important for young nobles to learn the social graces, as Castiglione described in *The Courtier*. The young earl of Essex, for example, began his school day at 7:00 A.M. with dancing lessons. Then, after breakfast, he studied French and Latin for an hour each. The next half hour was devoted to writing and drawing. After a period for prayers, recreation, and dinner, he had an hour-long science lesson. This was followed by more Latin, French, and writing. The school day ended at 5:30 with another session of prayers and recreation, then supper.

Elizabeth I followed a similar but even more rigorous program during her girlhood. Tutored by humanist professors from Cambridge University, she mastered ancient Greek and Latin, as well as French and Italian. In addition she learned to sing, dance, play musical instruments, write poetry, ride, and hunt. And her father realized that there was a chance she might one day rule England, so she was one Renaissance girl who did study—and master—the art of persuasive writing and public speaking.

Seven

CELEBRATIONS AND SPECTACLES

enaissance rulers had many cares and duties, but there was also time for recreation at court. Hunting on horseback with the assistance of hawks or hounds was a favorite activity. Another was court, or royal, tennis, which was played indoors in palaces and country homes. This sport was enjoyed by spectators as well as players. Quieter pastimes included card games (often played for high stakes), chess and other board games, playing or listening to music, and reading.

Dancing was a popular way to exercise as well as an art form and a social activity. It also had a philosophical meaning for many Renaissance people, who felt that the ordered movements of a dance reflected the harmony of nature and the universe. Some dances were slow and dignified, while others were quite energetic. For example, the galliard was so lively that when it was danced at balls, gentlemen were told to remove the swords they almost always wore at their sides. There is a Renaissance painting that shows Robert Dudley dancing a galliard

Two girls from a noble family of Cremona, Italy, play chess as their younger sister and a maid look on. This painting was made by the girls' oldest sister, Sofonisba Anguissola, whose artistic skills were well known and highly praised throughout Europe.

with Elizabeth I: as he takes a hopping or skipping step, he lifts the queen high into the air.

ROYAL ENTERTAINMENTS

On occasions such as birthdays, weddings, and visits from foreign rulers or ambassadors, Renaissance courts often presented theatrical spectacles called masques. These combined music, dancing, poetry, elaborate costumes, and "special effects." The performers were often lords and ladies of the court, but professional performers might be hired, too. The finest poets and composers provided scripts and music, and the best artists designed costumes, stages sets, and effects. For example, when Leonardo da Vinci was in France, he created a mechanical lion for one of King Francis I's masques. At the entertainment's climax, the lion opened and showered the audience with white lilies, the symbol of French royalty.

Many festivities featured fireworks. There were small fireworks displays for private gatherings and large ones for public celebrations. Duke Cosimo de' Medici organized elaborate displays for Florence's Feast of Saint John the Baptist. His fireworks were sometimes arranged in the shape of an ancient temple. Once they were set up to represent a scene from Dante's *Inferno,* the great thirteenth-century poem about a poet's journey through hell.

Mock battles, water shows, and processions were part of many courtly festivities. On a trip to the south of France, Catherine de' Medici held an elaborate riverside party that featured a ballet danced on a river island, a boat made to look like a whale, and a splendid banquet served by shepherdesses. Elizabeth I's coronation was marked by a magnificent procession. The queen, dressed in cloth of gold, was carried on a satin-draped litter and accompanied by an honor guard of gentlemen holding gilded battle-axes. The houses along the processional way were hung with colorful banners and tapestries. Wooden stages had been built at various points on the route. At each of these the queen stopped to watch a pageant of music and poetry presented in her honor.

FESTIVE FEASTS

Any celebration at court was bound to include at least one banquet. Sometimes a banquet would last nearly all day. Fish, fowl, and meat courses alternated with servings of salads and a selection of wines. At the end of the

Royal Foods to Enjoy Today

One result of European exploration in the Americas was the introduction of new foods, such as green beans and tomatoes. A New World dish often featured at Renaissance banquets was turkey. First brought from Mexico to Spain early in the sixteenth century, it quickly caught on as an exotic luxury food at courts all over Europe. At a banquet in Paris in 1549, Catherine de' Medici served sixty-six turkeys. The bird was prepared in many ways—boiled, roasted, accompanied by oysters, as an ingredient in pies, and so on—but cooks especially loved to serve it stuffed with a variety of meats and vegetables. One celebrated French recipe described turkey stuffed with Cornish hen, veal, bacon, mushrooms, and raspberries.

Another luxury that came to Renaissance courts from Mexico was chocolate. The explorer Hernán Cortés brought it to Spain in 1528 and served it to Emperor Charles V. Cortés prepared it in the Aztec way, as a drink that mixed water with unsweetened chocolate, cornstarch, hot peppers, allspice, and vanilla (another new food from the Americas). Before long, Europeans were making the drink with water, unsweetened chocolate, honey or sugar (a luxury from the Middle East), vanilla, cinnamon, and, occasionally, black pepper. Eventually they began to sometimes use milk instead of water. So the next time you have a glass of chocolate milk or a cup of hot chocolate, you might want to sprinkle a little cinnamon into it and imagine yourself at a royal Renaissance feast!

lengthy meal, diners enjoyed desserts and fruit. The goal of most banquets was to put on as splendid a display as possible. Giovanni Pontano, prime minister to the king of Naples, explained it this way: "Local and national dishes will not suffice, unless accompanied by many foodstuffs which appear to have been imported, with great difficulty, from abroad, so that a kind of deliberate variety, sought out with elaborate care, is apparent. . . . The courses themselves should be plentiful and varied; for variety adds much to the sumptuousness and provides great pleasure during the meal; and splendour and abundance are not readily evident without a number of courses."

The arrival of each course was announced by a trumpet fanfare. Musicians played during the meal, too, which both entertained the guests and kept the servants from talking. The best servants were silent and subtle—even though they often wore brightly colored livery, or uniforms—and could respond immediately to a diner's merest nod. Everyone behaved according to an exacting code of formal manners.

The banqueting hall was splendidly decorated with hangings on the walls and rugs on the floor. Plates and platters were of silver, gold, and the finest porcelain. In Italy, diners used two-pronged silver forks to eat their meat, salad, dessert, and fruit. The fork was an elegant refinement that had not yet caught on in the rest of Europe. Spoons, too, were still something of a luxury. Outside Italy, even at the most elaborate feasts, people ate mostly with knives and their fingers, and used bits of bread to mop up sauces and the like. Luckily, each diner was provided with a bowl of water, scented with rose petals or fragrant herbs, to wash hands between courses.

Eight

TROUBLED TIMES

In spite of the splendor and brilliance of Renaissance court life, these were difficult times in which to live. Epidemic diseases such as smallpox, cholera, and the plague affected all levels of society, including the highest. With limited medical knowledge and few effective medicines, even common illnesses and infections could be deadly. Death and misery were also caused by nearly constant warfare. Prejudice, suspicion, superstition, and greed brought their own brand of suffering to many in Europe's courts.

PLOTS IN HIGH PLACES

"Uneasy lies the head that wears a crown," wrote William Shakespeare in his play *Henry IV, Part 2*. Few Renaissance rulers felt completely secure on their thrones. They might be faced with rivals who claimed a better right to rule,

Everyone in Europe—rich and poor, young and old—was vulnerable to a great many diseases. This young man may be a victim of smallpox, leprosy, or the plague.

nobles who wished to overthrow them, territories that declared their independence, allies who betrayed them, and similar challenges. For example, Lorenzo de' Medici was trying to expand the power of Florence at the same time that Pope Sixtus IV was strengthening his power in the Papal States. Both leaders wanted to rule the town of Imola, and this began a feud that quickly heated up. The pope agreed to support a conspiracy against the Medici so that the rival Pazzi family could take control of Florence. On Easter Sunday, 1478, Lorenzo and his brother Giuliano were attacked during church. Giuliano was killed, but Lorenzo's escape from the conspirators resulted in a year and a half of warfare with the pope.

Some rulers lived in such terror of plots that they made themselves virtual prisoners in their own palaces. Most, however, continued to make public appearances, enjoy outdoor recreation, travel through their realms, and so on. They simply took precautions. Innkeepers were told to report any treasonous talk they might overhear, spies were sent to foreign courts, and suspected conspirators were closely watched. Naturally rulers also made sure to be well guarded by loyal soldiers and subjects. And the formal manners that decreed who was allowed to be where in a palace not only enhanced the dignity of court life but also gave the ruler an extra measure of security.

Shakespeare on Courts and Kings

William Shakespeare is regarded as England's greatest poet and playwright. He was also an actor, and began his career during the reign of Queen Elizabeth I. For almost twenty years, his acting company was sponsored by Elizabeth's lord chamberlain. The Lord Chamberlain's Men, as the company was known, sometimes entertained Elizabeth and her court. After the queen's death the company was renamed the King's Men, in honor of their new patron, King James I. Shakespeare's plays often featured characters who were kings, queens, and courtiers. Here and on the following pages are some of the things Shakespeare had to say about royalty and life at court.

There's such divinity doth hedge a king. . . .
—Hamlet, Act IV, Sc. 5

This portrait of Shakespeare, made for a shop sign, is thought to be a reasonable likeness of the great poet, capturing his intelligent and penetrating gaze.

The quality of mercy is not strained.
It droppeth as the gentle rain from heaven. . . .
'Tis mightiest in the mightiest. It becomes
The throned monarch better than his crown.
His sceptre shows the force of temporal power,
The attribute to awe and majesty,
Wherein doth sit the dread and fear of kings;
But mercy is above this sceptred sway.
It is enthroned in the hearts of kings;
It is an attribute to God himself,
And earthly power doth then show likest God's
When mercy seasons justice. . . .
—The Merchant of Venice, Act IV, Sc. 1

I think the King is but a man, as I am. The violet smells to him as it doth to me. . . .
All his senses have but human conditions. His ceremonies laid by, in his nakedness
he appears but a man, and though his affections are higher mounted than ours, yet
when they stoop, they stoop with the like wing. Therefore, when he sees reasons of
fears, as we do, his fears, out of doubt, be of the same relish as ours are.
—Henry V, Act IV, Sc. 1

. . . What infinite heartsease
Must kings neglect, that private men enjoy?
And what have kings that privates have not too,
Save ceremony, save general ceremony?
And what art thou, thou idol ceremony? . . .
Art thou aught else but place, degree, and form,
Creating awe and fear in other men?
Wherein thou art less happy, being feared,
Than they in fearing.
What drink'st thou oft, instead of homage sweet,
But poisoned flattery? . . .
. . . No, thou proud dream
That play'st so subtly with a king's repose;
I am a king that find thee, and I know
'Tis not the balm, the sceptre and the ball,
The sword, the mace, the crown imperial,
The intertissued robe of gold and pearl,
The farced title running 'fore the king,
The throne he sits on, nor the tide of pomp
That beats upon the high shore of this world—
No, not all these, thrice-gorgeous ceremony,
Not all these, laid in bed majestical,
Can sleep so soundlessly as the wretched slave. . . .
—*Henry V*, Act IV, Sc. 1

Gives not the hawthorn bush sweeter shade
To shepherds, looking on their seely [silly] sheep,
Than doth a rich embroidered canopy
To kings that fear their subjects' treachery?
—*Henry VI*, Part 3, Act III, Sc. 5

The Globe Theater, where many of Shakespeare's plays were first performed

For God's sake, let us sit upon the ground,
And tell sad stories of the death of kings—
How some have been deposed, some slain in war,
Some haunted by the ghosts they have deposed,
Some poisoned by their wives, some sleeping killed,
All murdered. For within the hollow crown
That rounds the mortal temples of a king
Keeps Death his court, and there the antic sits,
Scoffing his state and grinning at his pomp,
Allowing him a breath, a little scene,
To monarchize, be feared, and kill with looks,
Infusing him with self and vain conceit,
As if this flesh which walls about our life
Were brass impregnable; and humored thus,
Comes at the last, and with a little pin
Bores through his castle wall; and farewell, king.
—Richard II, Act III, Sc. 2

. . . we'll live,
And pray, and sing, and tell old tales, and laugh
At gilded butterflies, and hear poor rogues
Talk of our court news, and we'll talk with them too—
Who loses and who wins, who's in, who's out. . . .
—King Lear, Act V, Sc. 3

Vain pomp and glory of this world, I hate ye!
I feel my heart new opened. O, how wretched
Is that poor man that hangs on princes' favours!
—Henry VIII, Act III, Sc. 2

*Richard Tarlton, one of
Renaissance England's most
popular comic actors, playing a
pipe and tabor*

WARRING RELIGIONS

European rulers had always fought wars to conquer new territory, defend themselves, put down threats to their power, and the like. But the Renaissance saw the rise of a new cause of warfare. By the mid-sixteenth century, the Reformation had produced fierce hostilities among the powers of Europe. Some regions, especially Germany, were deeply torn apart as one portion of the population embraced Protestantism while another remained Catholic. It seemed that the two branches of Christianity had differences that could not be bridged, for the Catholic Church insisted on the absolute authority of the pope over all Christians. Protestants had

Some Protestant groups violently objected to the elaborate decoration of Catholic churches. This picture shows one such group smashing a church's stained-glass windows and pulling down its statues.

many differences among themselves, but all agreed in completely rejecting the pope's supremacy.

Protestant states and Catholic states saw each other as enemies. Perhaps even worse, there were often religious conflicts between rulers and their own subjects. The people of a country or city-state were generally expected to follow the religion of their ruler. This could lead to confusion at best, and tragedy at worst. When Ferdinand and Isabella conquered Muslim Granada in 1492, they forced all Muslims and Jews in Spain to either convert to Christianity or leave the country. After the Reformation, Spain did not tolerate Protestants within its borders either. And when Spanish adventurers began to conquer lands in the Americas, they were firmly instructed to take Catholic priests with them to convert the native people to Christianity.

Renaissance England provides another example of the effects religious conflict could have on a nation. When Martin Luther posted his Ninety-five Theses, King Henry VIII wrote such an eloquent response to the protest that the pope named him Defender of the Faith. Later, however, the pope refused to grant Henry's request for a divorce from his first wife. Henry rejected the pope's authority and founded the Church of England, with himself at its head. His son Edward VI, a sickly boy, upheld this new Protestant church during his short reign. Mary I, Henry's oldest daughter, then ascended the throne. She had remained a Catholic and was determined to reestablish Catholicism in England. The queen's persecutions of Protestants earned her the nickname Bloody Mary. She suspected that her sister, Elizabeth, was involved in a Protestant revolt and had her imprisoned. She was released only at Mary's death.

Elizabeth took the throne as a Protestant ruler, restoring the Church of England. Most English people supported her religious choice, for they looked on the pope as a foreign power. But like her father before her, Elizabeth faced revolts by Catholic nobles and executed some of them. There were also plots to put her Catholic cousin, Mary Queen of Scots, on the English throne. Spain, one of the staunchest Catholic countries, was backing many of the rebels against Elizabeth and was also making plans to invade England. As a result, practicing Catholicism could be regarded as an act of treason. Catholics were spied on and regarded with extreme suspicion. Some—especially men who went to other countries to become priests and then secretly returned to England—were tortured and executed as traitors. But Elizabeth basically tolerated Catholicism, so long as its followers remained loyal to her and practiced their faith quietly.

Another queen of the time, Catherine de' Medici, also struggled with religious issues. Catherine was a faithful Catholic, but she had great sympathy for France's Protestant minority—it filled her with pity and compassion to see them persecuted. Shortly after she became regent of France for her second son, she organized a discussion between Catholic and Protestant leaders. The next year she wrote an edict proclaiming tolerance for Protestantism. But then civil war broke out between France's Catholics and Protestants. Though Catherine made several attempts to bring about peace, the war raged for more than thirty years. Yet for the rest of her life, the queen continued to promote the idea that different religions must be able to coexist—diversity must be tolerated, for the peace, stability, and general good of the nation. It was a noble vision.

GLOSSARY

Burgundy during the Renaissance, a duchy (territory ruled by a duke or duchess) that included parts of northern and eastern France as well as present-day Belgium and the Netherlands

Catholic refers to the branch of Christianity under the authority of the pope

chancellor a ruler's secretary. The Lord Chancellor of England was head of the country's judicial system and presided over the House of Lords in Parliament.

convent common term for a women's monastery

courtier a person who lived at or regularly attended a ruler's court

dowry money, property, and goods supplied by a bride's family for her to bring into her marriage

fresco a wall painting made on fresh plaster

grammar to Renaissance humanists, the study of languages, especially ancient Greek and Latin

Holy Roman Empire an empire made up primarily of German, Austrian, and Italian territories, founded in A.D. 962 with the idea of unifying Europe

humanism an approach to learning that emphasized study of the subjects known as the humanities: grammar, rhetoric, literature, philosophy, and history

mercenary a soldier who fights only for money (as opposed to fighting out of loyalty to a country or cause)

monastery a religious institution where monks or nuns lived apart from the world, devoting themselves to prayer and study

monk a man who lived in a monastery, taking lifelong vows of poverty, chastity, and obedience

Muslim a follower of Islam, the religion founded in seventh-century Arabia by Muhammad

nun a woman who lived in a convent, taking lifelong vows of poverty, chastity, and obedience

Ottoman Empire empire based in Turkey, founded in the fourteenth century. At its peak in the 1500s it included North Africa, most of the Middle East, and part of southeastern Europe.

patron someone who gives financial support and other encouragement to an artist, musician, writer, etc.

Protestant refers to Christians who reject the authority of the pope and many practices and beliefs of the Catholic Church

Psalms a book of the Bible containing songlike poems of prayer and praise

Reformation the movement begun in 1517 by Martin Luther to reform the Catholic Church. Eventually the Reformation resulted in the founding of many different kinds of Christian groups, such as Lutherans, Anglicans (Episcopalians), Calvinists (Presbyterians), and Baptists.

regent a person who governs a territory on behalf of the official ruler, often because the ruler is too young or too sick to exercise authority

rhetoric the art of using language to persuade through eloquent speech or writing

FOR FURTHER READING

Ashby, Ruth. *Elizabethan England*. New York: Benchmark Books, 1999.

Caselli, Giovanni. *The Renaissance and the New World*. New York: Peter Bedrick, 1985.

Cole, Alison. *Renaissance*. London and New York: Dorling Kindersley, 2000.

Gallagher, Jim. *Sir Francis Drake and the Foundation of a World Empire*. Philadelphia: Chelsea House, 2001.

Greenblatt, Miriam. *Elizabeth I and Tudor England*. New York: Benchmark Books, 2002.

Halliwell, Sarah, ed. *The Renaissance: Artists and Writers*. Austin: Raintree Steck-Vaughn, 1998.

Howarth, Sarah. *Renaissance People*. Brookfield, CT: Millbrook Press, 1992.

————. *Renaissance Places*. Brookfield, CT: Millbrook Press, 1992.

Lassieur, Allison. *Leonardo da Vinci and the Renaissance in World History*. Berkeley Heights, NJ: Enslow Publishers, 2000.

Mann, Kenny. *Isabel, Ferdinand, and Fifteenth-Century Spain*. New York: Benchmark Books, 2002.

Matthews, Rupert. *The Renaissance*. New York: Peter Bedrick, 2000.

Merlo, Claudio. *Three Masters of the Renaissance: Leonardo, Michelangelo, Raphael*. Translated by Marion Lignana Rosenberg. Hauppauge, NY: Barron's Educational Series, 1999.

Millar, Heather. *Spain in the Age of Exploration*. New York: Benchmark Books, 1999.

Mühlberger, Richard. *What Makes a Leonardo a Leonardo?* New York: The Metropolitan Museum of Art/Viking, 1994.

Netzley, Patricia D. *Life During the Renaissance*. San Diego: Lucent Books, 1998.

Ruggiero, Adriane. *The Ottoman Empire*. New York: Benchmark Books, 2003.

Schomp, Virginia. *The Italian Renaissance*. New York: Benchmark Books, 2003.

Thomas, Jane Resh. *Behind the Mask: The Life of Queen Elizabeth I*. New York: Clarion Books, 1998.

Wood, Tim. *The Renaissance*. New York: Viking, 1993.

Yancey, Diane. *Life in the Elizabethan Theater*. San Diego: Lucent Books, 1997.

ON-LINE INFORMATION*

Annenberg/CPB. *Renaissance.*
   http://www.learner.org/exhibits/renaissance
The Artchive: Renaissance Art.
   http://artchive.com/artchive/renaissance.html
Chiarini, Gloria. *The Florence Art Guide.*
   http://www.mega.it/eng/egui/hogui.htm
History 254: Renaissance and Reformation Chronology.
   http://orb.rhodes.edu/schriber/chronology.html
Johnson, Phillip R. *The Hall of Church History: The Reformers.*
   http://www.gty.org/~phil/rformers.htm
Jokinen, Annilina. *16th Century Renaissance English Literature (1485–1603).*
   http://www.luminarium.org/renlit
Kren, Emil, and Daniel Marx. *Web Gallery of Art: Guided Tours.*
   http://gallery.euroweb.hu/tours/index.html
Matthews, Kevin. *Renaissance Architecture.*
   http://www.greatbuildings.com/types/styles/rcnaissance.html
Renaissance.
   http://renaissance.dm.net
Secara, Maggie. *Life in Elizabethan England: A Compendium of Common Knowledge.* Sixth edition, 2001.
   http://renaissance.dm.net/compendium/home.html
Shakespeare Resource Center.
   http://www.bardweb.net
Sites on Shakespeare and the Renaissance.
   http://web.uvic.ca/shakespeare/Annex/ShakSites1.html
Vatican Exhibit.
   http://www.ibiblio.org/cxpo/vatican.exhibit/Vatican.exhibit.html

*Websites change from time to time. For additional on-line information, check with the media specialist at your local library.

BIBLIOGRAPHY

Bell, Rudolph M. *How to Do It: Guides to Good Living for Renaissance Italians.* Chicago and London: University of Chicago Press, 1999.

Brown, Howard M. *Music in the Renaissance.* Englewood Cliffs, NJ: Prentice-Hall, 1976.

Editors of Time-Life Books. *What Life Was Like at the Rebirth of Genius: Renaissance Italy, AD 1400–1550.* Alexandria, VA: Time-Life Books, 1999.

————. *What Life Was Like in the Realm of Elizabeth: England AD 1533–1603.* Alexandria, VA: Time-Life Books, 1998.

Hale, John. *The Civilization of Europe in the Renaissance.* New York: Touchstone, 1993.

Jardine, Lisa. *Worldly Goods: A New History of the Renaissance.* New York: Doubleday, 1996.

Jardine, Lisa, and Jerry Brotton. *Global Interests: Renaissance Art between East and West.* Ithaca: Cornell University Press, 2000.

Johnson, Paul. *The Renaissance: A Short History.* New York: Modern Library, 2000.

Kekewich, Lucille, editor. *The Impact of Humanism.* New Haven and London: Yale University Press, 2000.

King, Margaret L. *Women of the Renaissance.* Chicago and London: University of Chicago Press, 1991.

Mateer, David, editor. *Courts, Poets, and Patrons.* New Haven and London: Yale University Press, 2000.

Rabb, Theodore. *Renaissance Lives: Portraits of an Age.* New York: Pantheon, 1993.

Rowse, A. L. *The Elizabethan Renaissance: The Life of the Society.* New York: Charles Scribner's Sons, 1971.

Shakespeare, William. *Complete Works, Compact Edition.* Edited by Stanley Wells et al. Oxford: Clarendon Press, 1988.

Wheaton, Barbara Ketcham. *Savoring the Past: The French Kitchen and Table from 1300 to 1789.* New York: Touchstone, 1996.

INDEX

Page numbers for illustrations are in boldface